THE WALK
TO THE
LIGHT

How to Change Your Life in 5 Steps

By: Corey D. Lillard

Copyright © 2024
All rights reserved.
No portion of this book may be reproduced in any form without written permission from the publisher or author, except as permitted by U.S. copyright law.
ISBN: 9798343422627
Independently published.

Dedicated to my daughters Anayah, Dyanni, Mariah, and my grandson Domani.

Preface

Welcome to *The Walk to the Light – Companion Guide: How to Change Your Life in 5 Steps*. As you start on this journey to transform your life, I want you to keep an open mind and heart about what lies ahead. In this guide, you'll find a roadmap to growing personally, recovering from tough times, and finding deep clarity in life, all of which lead to happiness.

Changing isn't easy. It requires guts, looking at yourself closely, and being ready to deal with your past. But through this journey of discovering yourself and making changes, you'll find the power to control your future and rewrite your story.

In *The Walk to the Light*, you'll go through five steps crucial for freeing yourself and feeling good all around. From changing your environment to building up supportive relationships, from changing how you think to taking care of your body, each step provides tips and tools to help you live a life custom to you with purpose.

As you read through these pages, I want you to keep an open mind and be curious. It might feel uncomfortable at times, but celebrate the moments you learn something new about yourself. Let the light inside you be a guide.

I hope this book gives you a new perception of life journey and inspiration as you transform your life. It should help you realize just how much potential you have, as well as the way to a future filled with clarity that will hopefully turn into happiness, purpose, and endless possibilities.

With gratitude and anticipation,
Corey

Contents

Preface i
Introduction 1

Part I: The 5 Steps

Chapter One: *Transform Your Environment for Personal Growth* .. 2
Chapter Two: *Liberation: Transform Your Mindset* 8
Chapter Three: *Transforming Your Behavior for a Fresh Start* ... 11
Chapter Four: *Having the Right Companion, Partner or Friend.* 13
Chapter Five: *Nurturing a Healthy Body: The Key to a Balanced Life* 15

Part II: Strategies for Motivation and Leadership

Chapter Six: *Striving for a Better Life* 19
Chapter Seven: *In Search of Familiar Love* 22
Chapter Eight: *Motivating People* 24
Chapter Nine: *Strong Leadership* 26
Chapter Ten: *The Importance of Being Determined* 28
Chapter Eleven: *The Importance of Believing in Yourself* 30
Chapter Twelve: *The Importance of Loving Yourself* 32
Chapter Thirteen: *Be Loyal to Your Goals* 34
Chapter Fourteen: *Focus on Your Goals* 35
Chapter Fifteen: *Staying Positive When Things Don't Go as Planned* 36
Chapter Sixteen: *My Speech to the People: The Power Is Within You* 38

CHAPTER SEVENTEEN: *Why Is Love Important?* 41
CHAPTER EIGHTEEN: *Staying Focused While Others Fight for Your Attention* 44
CHAPTER NINETEEN: *Why Some People Are Emotionally Unavailable* 47
CHAPTER TWENTY: *Motivation* 49
CHAPTER TWENTY-ONE: *How Faith Looks from a Strong Point of View* 51
ABOUT THE AUTHOR 53

Introduction

When you're trying to change yourself, it can feel stressful, discouraging, pointless, and impossible—like a big scary confusing mess. But that's where the magic happens! That's when you get to take control and make your life better. *The Walk to the Light* is here to enlighten you on the road to change and the darkness into the light that comes with it.

This book breaks it all down, which is challenging but worth every step. If you dive into each step with some serious thinking and commitment, you'll find the power to unlock and kickstart a journey to modify a new and improved you, which will lead to growth and happiness in your personal life.

This will help you have a new perception on life.

PART I

The 5 Steps

CHAPTER ONE
Transform Your Environment for Personal Growth

At a young age, I knew I had to do something differently with my life. However, the path to transformation appeared uncertain, because of the unknown roads and the unfamiliar rooms I had to endure. Also, while being consumed by past experiences and surrounded by individuals trapped in cycles of pain, living in survival mode.

This chapter explores the crucial first step toward change: reshaping one's surroundings and creating an environment is essential to personal growth. By embracing positivity, compassion, and supportive relationships, you can learn to navigate beyond the comfort of your past and present, cultivating a foundation for transformative growth.

* * *

At the age 27, I made a personal decision to reshape the path of my life, yet I struggled with where to start this journey of transformation. Along the path to change, also a new way of existence and thinking, I came to the realization that my personality and behavior were directly connected and formed from the life experiences I had accumulated up to that point of my life.

To venture towards a brighter future, I recognized the importance of identifying and overcoming the lessons and hardships of my past.

To build this new foundation for myself, it became clear I needed to put myself in an environment filled with positivity and compassion. I then learned to seek the company of individuals who would consistently promote personal growth and encourage me to become a better version of myself each day.

However, I found myself surrounded by people who, like me, had been shaped by a history of pain and were mentally trapped in survival mode. They were unaware of how the past had corrupted and altered their visions, personalities, and approaches to life.

Their existence was centered only on survival, and their pain had turned them into individuals who wanted to dominate and control others for their own selfish gain. This was the aftermath of their past, as well as my own.

I came to understand that genuine transformation does not occur through seeking dominance but through embracing equal rights. This realization propelled me toward change and prepared me for this transformation.

I needed the support of others who were willing to acknowledge the past while remaining dedicated to focusing on the future. It is a common human tendency to navigate life by constantly glancing in the rearview mirror, using the past as a guide for our present actions.

However, to mold our future in a more positive light, we must develop the capacity to see beyond the past and present. To equip yourself for this challenging change, you must surround yourself with like-minded individuals who offer love and support.

Chapter Two
Liberation: Transform Your Mindset

I will discuss the journey to personal freedom by examining your thoughts and understanding how your past influences your actions and relationships. By reflecting deeply on yourself and shifting your perspective, you can begin to live more honestly and treat yourself and others with greater kindness.

This section of the book provides guidance on breaking free from outdated mindsets and embracing a new, happier version of yourself.

* * *

To liberate my mind and adjust my attitude, I envisioned myself on a journey of self-discovery, seeking a life different from the one I had witnessed during my upbringing. I closely observed the lives of those around me, analyzing their actions, how they were perceived by others, and the emotions they expressed to their audiences.

What I often saw was a sense of selfishness. People seemed to invest in each other for personal gain, engaging in manipulation and backstabbing when necessary. The love I had hoped to find appeared distant, replaced by toxic relationships lacking compassion for others. This toxic love not only conditioned us to be used and manipulated but also altered our perception of how love should be received.

As I observed the lives of those around me, I realized I was not only peering into their pasts but also my own. We shared the same rearview mirror, and by examining their actions, I reflected on my own. To manifest this change, I needed to understand my roots and where I had come from.

Every action I witnessed seemed to revolve around survival. It felt as if our lives depended on every decision and action we made, constantly struggling to stay afloat in a turbulent sea. Survival had become our way of life, consuming our existence.

To adjust my attitude, I had to transition from simply surviving to truly living. I needed to embrace a way of life that honored me and respected those who had invested in me. I searched for and prayed to discover a new way of being.

These realizations about my past experiences and their impact on my identity initially plunged me into a state of depression. I struggled with feelings of weakness and questioned whether I had allowed myself to be taken advantage of. I wondered how many people I had unintentionally hurt along the way on this path called life.

However, I soon realized I did not need to inflict self-blame. The trials of my upbringing left scars, but they also created a force of resilience. I had weathered the storm, and I was now ready for change.

Acknowledging and accepting your past is like shining a light into your own mind. It's the first step in transforming your mindset and taking deliberate steps toward positive change instead of dwelling in darkness.

During this transformative period, I learned to love the world and people in an extremely different way—a way that truly liberated my spirit. It felt as though I had taken the chains that once tied me down, hindering me, and used them to propel myself into a new and better life. This was the body of liberation.

Chapter Three
Transforming Your Behavior for a Fresh Start

———⸻———

Building on your newfound free-thinking mindset, this chapter helps you explore practical ways to change your behavior. It focuses on recognizing your repeated patterns and experimenting with new approaches. By doing so, you'll gain deeper self-awareness and begin to transform into a whole new person.

This section of the book encourages you to disrupt your usual routines, embrace discomfort, and try activities that push you out of your comfort zone. It's all about taking the required steps to align with the new you that you're discovering.

* * *

Once you've addressed the initial steps in this journey, changing your behavior becomes more manageable. I had to accept that what I perceived as boring or purposeless activities only felt that way because they didn't fit into my past life story. When living in survival mode, your choice of activities is different. Those who have endured a challenging past often find comfort in familiar routines, regardless of the consequences.

To embrace my new path successfully, I needed to adjust how I carried myself. This adjustment didn't mean altering my core identity but rather finding a balance between the survival instincts ingrained in me and a perspective more aligned with my new way of life.

I also had to identify activities that I enjoyed but weren't beneficial and which I had gravitated towards because of my past. It meant discovering new interests and hobbies. Undoubtedly, breaking lifelong habits and exploring new behaviors can be challenging and, at times, frightening. However, it is precisely these changes that make all the difference when you are striving to transform your life.

Use the inner strength you've cultivated through your life experiences to dismantle any behaviors keeping you stagnant. Every action you take, every decision you make, should propel you forward.

Introducing more discomfort into a life already damaged by pain might seem insane. Yet, by placing yourself in different settings, among diverse people, and embracing new behaviors, you'll come to realize stepping out of your comfort zone is essential for finding the path toward enlightenment—a path that leads to a new and improved way of living.

Chapter Four
Having the Right Companion, Partner or Friend

This chapter emphasizes the crucial role of supportive friends and partners in your journey of self-transformation. It highlights the importance of surrounding yourself with people who share your vision and uplift you.

By building relationships with individuals who inspire and encourage you, you can grow into a better version of yourself. Whether you're working through past issues or striving to be more open with others, these meaningful connections can significantly help in your personal development.

* * *

Having the right companion, partner, or friend is crucial in your journey toward change. If you choose someone who is unwilling to evolve or support your transformation, you risk remaining stuck in your past.

Many individuals shape their lives by reflecting on and living out their past experiences, and not all are willing to shift their focus forward. If your companion, partner, or friend cannot spare the time to divert their attention from their own past and acknowledge yours, then they will be unable to assist you in your quest for progress. It is crucial to have someone who recognizes you for who you are and is wholeheartedly committed to aiding you on your journey.

Your companion, partner, or friend should consistently inspire you to become a better version of yourself each day, but they must also understand your comfort is critical for progress. Change is extremely challenging, and there are moments when you need to pause and appreciate the present. You must also be able to discern when you need some personal space to relax, and it is important to have a companion, partner, or friend who respects that need.

Being in a relationship or friendship with someone entangled in their own past or unwilling to support your growth will only lead you into darkness. The path to transformation is difficult, and having to drag someone along with you can make it feel nearly impossible.

In clarity, seek out a companion, partner, or friend who serves as a positive force in your life, mutually pushing each other to become better versions of yourselves with each passing day.

Chapter Five
Nurturing a Healthy Body: The Key to a Balanced Life

This chapter highlights the essential role of physical well-being in your overall self-transformation. It covers the importance of proper nutrition, regular exercise, and dedicated self-care. By nurturing your body, you provide yourself with the energy and strength needed for growth and success.

Recognizing the connection of mind, body, and spirit allows you to achieve a pleasant balance, leading to a greater sense of well-being. Therefore, prioritizing your physical health becomes a foundation of feeling truly great—inside and out.

* * *

The life and energy of your body and the resilience of your mind are deeply interconnected; one cannot thrive without the other. Over the past 17 years, I have dedicated my life to health and wellness. As the youngest of six siblings, I took on the responsibility of caring for my father for thirteen years.

During this journey, I had a heartfelt realization. While family and friends may offer their utmost support, there comes a point when you must become your own pillar of strength. I understood I needed to provide myself with the best opportunities to flourish and improve, even without the support of others.

But what does it mean to truly take care of oneself? While I've extensively discussed the mental aspects of effecting change, what choices can you make to nourish your body and mind for the journey ahead?

Loving yourself first, proper nutrition, regular exercise, and the proper amount of sleep—these seemingly small choices provide the energy needed to elevate yourself mentally and emotionally, propelling you toward new levels of life.

If your goal is self-improvement across all facets of existence, you should prioritize the well-being of your body as much as you prioritize your mental health.

* * *

As you wrap up this journey of self-transformation, remember you are not alone. We are all on this path together, striving to grow and improve.

In these final reflections, acknowledge the challenges and achievements you've encountered, and remain faithful in your commitment to self-improvement.

Keep focusing on your path forward, for a brighter, happier future awaits you.

PART II

Strategies for Motivation and Leadership

Chapter Six
Striving for a Better Life

Each day brings familiar emotions as I march forward in my quest to become the best version of myself. It's strange that many in my circle treat me the same, despite my efforts to improve. I've come to realize growth can be a painful process for some people. My life is a constant journey of seeking skills to enhance my existence, consistently rejecting bitterness, and focusing on positive improvements.

When I speak with strength and love, it often challenges those around me, evoking unwanted feelings because true love can be uncomfortable. Many of us were taught to love conditionally—to shelter our feelings by not challenging us and only telling us what we want to hear.

By not attaching to these conditions, people tend to look for weaknesses in my life or fabricate false stories about me. These perceived flaws become weapons to use against me, intending to project the same unwanted feelings they experience. What they fail to understand is that I am well aware of my imperfections, and I know each weakness requires time and effort to transform. I take one step at a time to strengthen these aspects of myself.

To maintain my focus, I remain extremely aware of my journey, alert that personal growth can make those around me uncomfortable. Simply being in my presence may lead people to reflect on their own unhealthy behaviors, which can bring forth a feeling of being attacked. When individuals feel attacked, their natural instinct strikes back, often targeting known or perceived weaknesses.

Living a life like mine, without understanding, can be frustrating. When people are unaware, their emotional reactions can lead them to highlight your vulnerabilities constantly. However, I have a deep understanding of my shortcomings because I can sense the discomfort when I confront these areas. I refuse to allow anyone to use my weaknesses to undermine my potential or dictate my future.

To those who may strike out at me, I extend love and empathy. I understand the pain that accompanies unwanted feelings and the tendency to react defensively. This defensive reaction often triggers similar responses from others, creating a cycle of hurt and a lack of empathy.

My mission is to break this pattern. I acknowledge the pain my presence may cause and the discomfort that growth can bring. Despite any attacks born from emotions and real-time life pressures, I will continue to offer love and support. I recognize it's not the person but the pain itself that takes over.

To all who hope for greatness in their lives, I encourage you to remain focused and aware of the discomfort, emotions, and pain that often accompany personal growth. I aim to inspire hope in those around me and refuse to be shaped by the actions of others. Blessings to all.

CHAPTER SEVEN
In Search of Familiar Love

Like my mother, I often found myself seeking love in the eyes of others, only to be disappointed by the pain and scars of the past that have shaped them. My life has been a constant effort to understand and justify the pain inflicted upon me by exploring the pasts of those who hurt me. My heart has been wounded since my earliest memories, both by the actions of others and my own mistakes. When you encounter pain consistently, you grow accustomed to its presence.

I'm on a mission to show people there's a better way. In a world where pain seems to surround us, it's disheartening to witness so much suffering. Sometimes, we're left with no choice but to choose from the options presented to us, hoping to find someone who truly fits into our lives.

I refuse to settle, even if it means enduring loneliness for a while. My kindness extends to everyone, and I strive to help all I can. I often wonder if pain is an inevitable part of life and if I'll always have to endure hurt from those I love.

The Walk to the Light – Companion Guide

I frequently ponder whether I was created to understand people's ways, having witnessed what pain did to my parents and those from my past. I find myself skeptical about how most people love. Both of my parents sought comfort from their pain by loving those they could relate to, which ultimately led to their downfall. My father chose the path of conflict, hurting those who invested in him. My mother chose the path of unconditional love, absorbing the pain others directed her way until it consumed her.

Over time, alcohol became my mother's comfort, causing her to only share love with those who reciprocated the energy of her tolerance. Mixing good with bad often yields negative outcomes, and my mother lost her forgiving love, much like my father. Pain destroyed them both.

Here I stand, bearing a heart similar to my past, offering help and love to the very people who inflict pain upon me. I accept their flawed ways because I can relate to them. My past was marked by pain, which my heart has grown accustomed to. I fear the vision of darkness because I see so much light.

I ask myself if the reason I welcome people into my life who share my past pain is because I believe that together, we can help others overcome the pain we've experienced, or perhaps it's because I feel a sense of belonging with them. These thoughts weigh heavily on me—to overcome, to love, to be set free.

Chapter Eight
Motivating People

Motivating people who are living in struggle and pain but want to live better can be challenging, but here are some strategies that may be helpful:

Empathize

It's essential to understand the struggles and pain that the person is experiencing. By acknowledging and validating their feelings, you can build trust and create a safe space for them to open up.

Listen

People often feel motivated when they feel heard and understood. Take the time to actively listen to their concerns and goals without judgment.

Offer Support

Let them know you're there to support them, whether it's

through emotional support, active assistance, or connecting them with resources that can help.

ENCOURAGE SMALL STEPS

Breaking down large goals into smaller, more manageable tasks can make them feel less stressed. Celebrate their progress, no matter how small, and help them stay focused on the next step.

SHARE SUCCESS STORIES

Sharing success stories of others who have overcome similar struggles can be inspiring and give hope to those who are struggling.

FOCUS ON THE POSITIVE

Encourage them to focus on the positive aspects of their lives, no matter how small, and help them see the possibilities for a better future.

HELP THEM FIND PURPOSE

Help them identify their values and goals and find ways to connect them with activities that align with these values. Having a sense of purpose can be a powerful motivator.

Remember, motivation is a personal journey, and what works for one person may not work for another. It's essential to tailor your approach to each individual and work with them to find what motivates them best.

CHAPTER NINE
Strong Leadership

We all know strong leadership is essential in many aspects of our lives, whether in business, politics, or community organizations. In today's world, where we face numerous challenges and uncertainties, the need for strong and effective leadership has never been greater.

Leadership is the ability to inspire, guide, and influence others to work towards a common goal. A strong leader has the ability to bring people together and make them feel motivated and committed to achieving a shared objective. Strong leadership is crucial for any organization or community to thrive, as it provides direction, guidance, and inspiration to its members.

In business, strong leadership is the key to success. A strong leader can motivate employees, create a positive work environment, and guide the organization towards achieving its objectives.

In politics, strong leadership is essential for the well-being of society. A leader who is honest, visionary, and compassionate can inspire the people and lead them towards a better future. Strong leadership can also help to bring different groups and communities together and build unity around important issues.

In community organizations, strong leadership can bring people together to work towards a common cause. A leader who is passionate, committed, and empathetic can create a sense of togetherness and purpose among members and help to achieve their shared goals.

In conclusion, strong leadership is critical in many aspects of our lives. A strong leader can inspire, guide, and influence others towards achieving a shared objective. Strong leadership is essential for businesses, politics, and community organizations to thrive and adapt to changing circumstances.

Let us all strive to be strong leaders in our own lives and work towards creating a better future for ourselves and those around us.

Chapter Ten
The Importance of Being Determined

Determination is the quality that separates those who achieve their goals from those who simply dream about them. It is the fuel that propels us towards our objectives, even in the face of challenges and setbacks.

When we are determined, we are willing to put in the work, to push through the difficult times, and to make sacrifices in order to achieve our dreams. We don't give up when we encounter obstacles, we don't quit when we fail, and we don't let fear or doubt hold us back.

Determination is what sets successful people apart from those who simply coast through life. It is what drives athletes to train for hours every day, what pushes entrepreneurs to work tirelessly to build their businesses, and what motivates students to study late into the night.

The power of determination can be seen in countless stories of individuals who overcame incredible obstacles to achieve their goals. But determination is not just for the famous and accomplished. Each and every one of us has the power to be determined in our own lives, to set our sights on our goals, and to work tirelessly to achieve them. Whether it's excelling in our careers, pursuing a passion, or overcoming a personal challenge, we all have the ability to be determined and make our dreams a reality.

So, I encourage each and every one of you to embrace determination in your own lives. Set your sights on your goals, be willing to work hard, and don't let setbacks or obstacles discourage you. With determination, anything is possible, and you have the power to achieve your dreams.

Chapter Eleven
The Importance of Believing in Yourself

Believing in yourself is crucial for personal growth, achievement, and happiness. When you believe in yourself, you have confidence in your abilities and potential, which can help you overcome obstacles, take risks, and pursue your goals.

Here are some key reasons why believing in yourself is important:

Self-confidence:

When you believe in yourself, you have a strong sense of self-confidence, which can help you navigate challenges and difficult situations. It can also help you make better decisions and take risks that lead to personal and professional growth.

Self-esteem

Believing in yourself can also boost your self-esteem, which is important for mental health and wellbeing. When you feel good about yourself, you are more likely to have a positive outlook on life and feel satisfied with your accomplishments.

Resilience

Believing in yourself can help you become more resilient in the face of adversity. It can help you bounce back from setbacks and stay motivated to pursue your goals, even when faced with obstacles.

Inspiration

When you believe in yourself, you can inspire others to believe in themselves as well. Your confidence and positive attitude can be contagious and can help motivate others to pursue their own goals and dreams.

So, trust in yourself and your abilities, and pursue your dreams with confidence and determination.

Chapter Twelve
The Importance of Loving Yourself

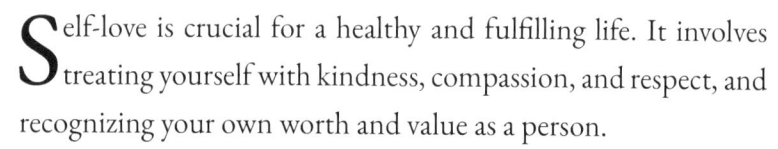

Self-love is crucial for a healthy and fulfilling life. It involves treating yourself with kindness, compassion, and respect, and recognizing your own worth and value as a person.

When you love yourself, you are better able to set boundaries, make decisions that align with your values and goals, and feel confident and secure in who you are. This can lead to increased happiness and well-being, as well as better relationships with others.

Additionally, self-love can help prevent negative self-talk and self-criticism. When you love and accept yourself, you are less likely to engage in harmful self-criticism or compare yourself to others. Instead, you are more likely to focus on your strengths and positive qualities, and approach challenges and mistakes with a growth mindset.

However, self-love can be difficult to cultivate, especially if you have experienced trauma or have been subjected to toxic messages about yourself. But with practice and patience, it is pos-

The Walk to the Light – Companion Guide

sible to build a strong foundation of self-love. This can involve engaging in self-care activities you enjoy, practicing gratitude and positive affirmations, and seeking support from trusted friends and family members.

Self-love is an essential component of a happy and fulfilling life. It can help you to feel confident, resilient, and fulfilled, and can improve your relationships with others. So, start today by treating yourself with kindness and compassion, and cultivate a love for yourself that will serve you for a lifetime.

Chapter Thirteen
Be Loyal to Your Goals

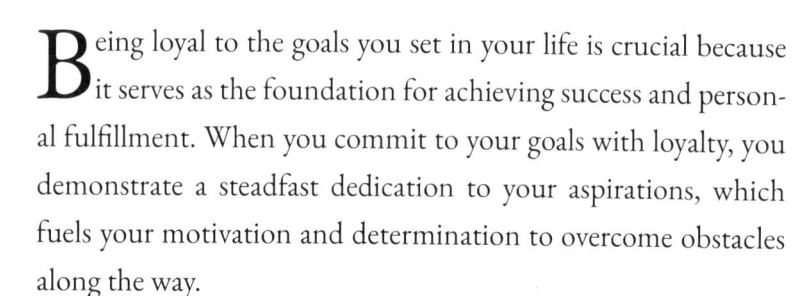

Being loyal to the goals you set in your life is crucial because it serves as the foundation for achieving success and personal fulfillment. When you commit to your goals with loyalty, you demonstrate a steadfast dedication to your aspirations, which fuels your motivation and determination to overcome obstacles along the way.

Loyalty keeps you focused and resilient, even when faced with challenges or setbacks, as it instills a sense of responsibility and accountability to see your goals through to fulfillment. In addition, staying loyal to your goals creates consistency and discipline, essential qualities for making progress and achieving your dreams over time.

Ultimately, loyalty to your goals empowers you to stay true to yourself, your values, and your aspirations, guiding you toward a life of purpose and accomplishment.

Chapter Fourteen
Focus on Your Goals

Focusing on your goals is important for several reasons:

Clarity: By defining your goals and focusing on them, you gain clarity about what you want to achieve. This clarity helps you make better decisions, prioritize your tasks, and stay on track towards achieving your desired outcome.

Motivation: When you focus on your goals, you create a sense of purpose and motivation that can drive you towards success. You'll be more likely to work hard and stay committed, even when faced with obstacles or setbacks.

Accountability: Focusing on your goals helps you hold yourself accountable for your progress. By regularly checking in on your progress, you can adjust your approach and make necessary changes to stay on track.

Achievement: Ultimately, focusing on your goals helps you achieve them. By staying committed, motivated, and accountable, you increase your chances of success and can reach your desired outcome more quickly and efficiently.

In summary, focusing on your goals ultimately helps you achieve what you set out to accomplish.

CHAPTER FIFTEEN
Staying Positive When Things Don't Go as Planned

Staying positive when things don't go as planned can be challenging, but it's essential for maintaining a healthy mindset and continuing to move forward. Here are some tips to help you stay positive in the face of setbacks:

PRACTICE GRATITUDE

Take a moment to appreciate what you do have, even if things haven't gone as planned. Consider the things in your life you are grateful for and focus on those instead of dwelling on what went wrong.

REFRAME YOUR THOUGHTS

Instead of focusing on the negative aspects of the situation, try to reframe your thoughts in a positive light. For example, instead of saying "I failed," try saying "I learned something from this experience that will help me in the future."

Stay Present

Don't let worries about the past or future consume you. Instead, focus on the present moment and what you can do to move forward from here.

Take Action

Rather than feeling helpless or defeated, take action to address the situation. Break down the problem into smaller steps and focus on what you can do right now to move forward.

Surround Yourself with Positivity

Spend time with people who uplift you and support you and engage in activities that bring you joy and fulfillment. Remember that setbacks and failures are a natural part of life, and they can provide valuable opportunities for growth and learning.

By staying positive and focusing on the good, you can overcome challenges and emerge stronger than ever before.

Chapter Sixteen
My Speech to the People: The Power Is Within You

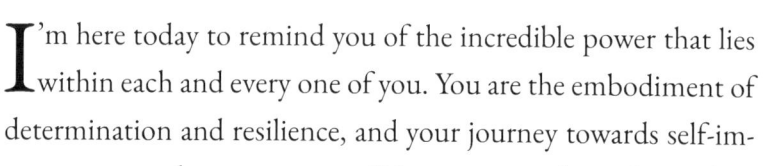

I'm here today to remind you of the incredible power that lies within each and every one of you. You are the embodiment of determination and resilience, and your journey towards self-improvement and greater accomplishments is nothing short of remarkable. Life can be a challenging and difficult road, but it is your decided spirit that makes all the difference.

In your pursuit of personal growth and the mission to achieve your dreams, remember you are not alone. Each step you take, each obstacle you overcome, is a testament to your inner strength and the relentless pursuit of your goals. It's easy to get discouraged, to feel overwhelmed, and to question whether your efforts are truly worth it. But let me assure you, they absolutely are.

Life is not just about the destination; it's about the journey as well. Every challenge you face, every setback you endure, is an opportunity to grow stronger, wiser, and more resilient. It's these struggles that will shape you into the person you were meant to be. Embrace them, learn from them, and use them as stepping-stones towards a brighter future.

The road to success is never a straight line. It's filled with twists, turns, and unexpected detours. But it's in these moments of uncertainty that your true character is revealed. It's when you face adversity head-on that you realize your full potential. Your ability to persevere, rise above the obstacles, and keep going is what sets you apart from the rest.

So, when life knocks you down—and it will—don't stay down. Get up with the fire of determination burning in your heart. Remember, every setback is just a setup for a comeback. Take those failures and turn them into valuable lessons. Use them as fuel to propel yourself even further towards your goals.

Believe in yourself, for you are stronger than you think. Your potential knows no limits. You are capable of achieving greatness, and your dreams are well within your reach. Trust in your journey, for the path you are on is uniquely yours.

Surround yourself with positivity, with people who believe in you and your vision. Let their faith in you fuel your determination. And remember, the only person you ever need to prove anything to is yourself. Your growth is a personal journey, and your accomplishments are a testament to your own strength and resilience.

As you continue to strive for greatness, keep your dreams alive in your heart and your goals at the forefront of your mind. Visualize your success and believe in your ability to achieve it. The world is full of opportunities waiting for you to seize them.

So, my friends, in those moments when the weight of the world feels heavy and the journey seems long, never forget the strong spirit within you. Keep going, keep pushing forward, and never lose sight of the incredible person you are becoming.

Together, we will overcome every obstacle, shatter every limitation, and rise to new heights. The world is yours for the taking, and you have the strength and determination to make your mark upon it. Keep going, and let your journey inspire the world.

Thank you, and may your relentless pursuit of greatness continue to light the way for all.

Chapter Seventeen
Why Is Love Important?

Love is important for several reasons, and its significance can be seen in various aspects of human life and well-being:

Emotional Well-Being: Love—whether it's romantic love, family love, or love between friends—contributes significantly to our emotional well-being. It provides a sense of belonging, security, and support, which can lead to increased happiness and reduced stress.

Social Connection: Love forms the foundation of social connections and relationships. It helps people bond and connect with others, fostering a sense of community, cooperation, and shared experiences.

Mental Health: Love plays a crucial role in mental health. Feeling loved and supported can reduce feelings of loneliness, anxiety, and depression. It provides a sense of purpose and motivation to maintain one's mental well-being.

Physical Health: Love can have positive effects on physical health. Research has shown that people in loving relationships tend to live longer, have lower blood pressure, and experience improved immune system functioning. This is often referred to as the "love effect."

Personal Growth: Love can inspire personal growth and development. When we love and are loved, we are more likely to take risks, try new things, and work towards self-improvement. Love can motivate individuals to become the best versions of themselves.

Empathy and Compassion: Love is closely linked to empathy and compassion. It encourages us to understand and care for the feelings and needs of others, promoting kindness and cooperation in society.

Family and Relationships: Love is the foundation of strong, healthy family relationships. It provides the emotional glue that holds families together, helping parents nurture and raise children and enabling children to form secure attachments.

Human Connection: Love is a fundamental part of the human experience. It defines our most meaningful connections and experiences. It's a source of joy, satisfaction, and meaning in our lives.

Love: Love for others often motivates acts of kindness and charity. People who care about the well-being of others are more likely to engage in acts of kindness and contribute to the betterment of society.

Sense of Purpose: Love, whether it's love for a person, a cause, or a passion, can give individuals a sense of purpose and direction in life. It motivates them to work towards something they deeply care about.

In summary, love is important because it contributes to our emotional, social, and physical well-being, fosters positive human connections, and inspires personal and societal growth. It's a fundamental and essential aspect of the human experience.

Chapter Eighteen
Staying Focused While Others Fight for Your Attention

Staying focused when other people are demanding your attention can be challenging, but it's certainly possible with some strategies and self-discipline. Here are some tips to help you stay focused:

Set Clear Goals: Know what you want to accomplish and set clear, specific goals. Having a clear purpose will help you stay on track even when distractions arise.

Prioritize Tasks: Use a to-do list or task management system to prioritize your tasks. Focus on the most important and urgent tasks first and allocate your attention accordingly.

Time Management: Allocate specific blocks of time for focused work. For example, you might dedicate the first hour of your workday to your most important task with no interruptions.

Create a Distraction-Free Environment: Minimize distractions in your workspace. Put your phone on silent or in another room, close unnecessary browser tabs, and let others know

The Walk to the Light – Companion Guide

when you need uninterrupted time.

Use Headphones: If you're in a shared space and can't control the noise, consider using noise-canceling headphones. They can help drown out background noise and signal to others that you're focused on a task.

Communicate Your Needs: Be open with the people around you. Let them know when you need focused time to work on a specific task. Setting boundaries and expectations can reduce interruptions.

Practice Mindfulness: Mindfulness techniques can help you stay present and focused. Meditation, deep breathing exercises, or even short breaks to stretch and refocus your mind can be beneficial.

Chunk Your Work: Break your work into smaller, more manageable chunks. Focus on completing one chunk at a time and use short breaks in between to check messages or address other people's needs.

Use Productivity Tools: There are various apps and tools designed to help you stay focused and manage your time better. Tools like timers or website blockers can be particularly useful.

Learn to Say No: It's important to say no to requests or distractions that aren't aligned with your current goals or tasks. Politely decline and explain that you need to focus on your work.

Practice Discipline: Building discipline takes time, but it's essential for maintaining focus. Remind yourself of your goals and the importance of staying on task.

Reflect and Adjust: Regularly assess your focus strategies and make adjustments as needed. What works for one person may not work for another, so be willing to experiment and find what works best for you.

Take Care of Your Health: Ensure you're getting enough sleep, staying hydrated, and eating well. Physical well-being can significantly impact your ability to concentrate.

Remember that maintaining focus is a skill that can be developed over time. It may take some practice and experimentation to find the strategies that work best for you in different situations. Be patient with yourself and keep refining your approach as needed.

Chapter Nineteen
Why Some People Are Emotionally Unavailable

There can be various reasons why some people may be emotionally unavailable. It's important to note that each individual is unique, and their emotional availability can be influenced by a combination of factors. Here are a few possible explanations:

Past Experiences: People who have experienced significant emotional pain or trauma in their past may develop emotional walls as a defense mechanism. They might fear vulnerability and intimacy due to the fear of getting hurt again.

Fear of Rejection or Abandonment: Some individuals may have deep-seated fears of being rejected or abandoned, which can make them emotionally distant. They may choose to keep their emotions guarded as a way to protect themselves from potential pain.

Attachment Style: People with certain attachment styles, such as avoidant attachment, may struggle with emotional intimacy. They may have learned to suppress their emotions or maintain a sense of independence as a result of early life experiences.

Personal Beliefs and Values: Some individuals may hold beliefs or values that prioritize self-reliance, independence, or emotional detachment. They might perceive emotional vulnerability as a sign of weakness or view emotional connections as unnecessary.

Mental Health Issues: Conditions like depression, anxiety, or personality disorders can affect a person's emotional availability. These individuals may find it challenging to engage in healthy emotional connections due to their own internal struggles.

Poor Relationship Role Models: Growing up in an environment where emotional intimacy was lacking or where relationships were unhealthy can shape a person's ability to be emotionally available. They might not have learned how to express or navigate emotions effectively.

It's important to remember that emotional availability is not necessarily a permanent trait. Some individuals may be temporarily emotionally unavailable due to life circumstances, while others may work through their barriers and become more open over time.

Understanding and empathy can play a crucial role in fostering emotional connection, but it's also important to respect the boundaries of individuals who may need space or time to address their emotional availability.

Chapter Twenty
Motivation

We all come from different walks of life, with different dreams and aspirations, but today, we stand united for one common goal: to create a better world for ourselves and the future generations.

We have all faced challenges in life—whether it be financial, social, or personal. But what separates us from the rest is our resilience and determination to overcome these obstacles. We have the power to create the change we want to see in the world. The power to shape our lives and the lives of others.

But let's not forget, the journey to a better life requires a lot of hard work and determination. We must be willing to fight for what we believe in, never give up, and always keep pushing forward. We must never be afraid to challenge the circumstances and stand up for what is right, even if it means going against the norm.

Together, we can create a world where everyone has equal opportunities, where everyone has access to education, healthcare, and a good life. A world where everyone is respected, regardless of their race, gender, or background. A world where love and kindness are valued over hate and division.

So, my dear friends, let us not be complacent with the way things are. Let us fight for a better life, not only for ourselves but for those who come after us. Let us work together to create a world that is just, fair, and equitable for all.

In conclusion, I would like to remind you of the words of Dr. Martin Luther King Jr., who said, "The time is always right to do what is right." Let us be the change we want to see in the world. Let us fight for a better life, for a better world.

Thank you!

Chapter Twenty-One
How Faith Looks from a Strong Point of View

Ladies and gentlemen,

Today, I will discuss a topic that transcends pure belief—it is the essence of strength, resilience, and unwavering conviction. I speak of faith, not merely as a passive acceptance, but as a force that propels us forward, even in the face of adversity.

From a strong point of view, faith is not blind trust; it is a conscious choice to believe in something greater than ourselves. It is the unwavering belief in our ability to overcome challenges, achieve our goals, and create a better future. Faith empowers us to take bold risks, knowing that even if we stumble, we will rise again, stronger than before.

True faith is not shaken by doubt or fear; it stands firm in the face of uncertainty and chaos. It is the anchor that keeps us grounded when the storms of life rage around us. Faith does not guarantee a smooth journey, but it provides us with the courage and strength to navigate the rough waters and emerge victorious on the other side.

In addition, faith is not a solitary pursuit; it is strengthened by community and connection. When we come together in shared belief and purpose, our faith becomes an unstoppable force for positive change. It inspires us to lift each other up, support one another, and work towards a common vision of a brighter future for all.

Concluding, faith from a strong point of view is not passive or weak—it is bold, resilient, and unwavering. It is the driving force behind our greatest achievements and the source of our inner strength in times of trial. So let us embrace faith not as a fleeting hope, but as a solid ground conviction that fuels our journey towards a better tomorrow.

> Love,
> The Walk to the Light

About the Author

Corey Damond Lillard was born and raised in East Oakland, California, as the youngest of eight siblings. From a young age, he faced a series of life-altering events that would test his resilience and shape his future. At just eight years old, Corey was involved in a traumatic motorcycle accident that left him unconscious and required immediate surgery. This early brush with mortality was just the beginning of the trials he would face.

By the age of eleven, Corey became a victim of gun violence, shot at point-blank range. The attack left him hospitalized for six months, during which he underwent six major surgeries to repair the damage. The physical pain was immense, but the emotional toll of surviving such a brutal attack was even greater. Yet, through the darkness, Corey began to cultivate an inner strength that would eventually guide his life's purpose.

Corey's childhood was also deeply affected by witnessing domestic violence in his home. His mother, a woman he admired for her strength, was repeatedly subjected to abuse at the hands of her partner. Tragically, this violence and alcohol abuse would claim her life when Corey was only thirteen. Losing his mother under such heartbreaking circumstances could have broken his spirit, but instead, it fueled his determination to rise above his surroundings.

Despite these devastating experiences, Corey refused to be defined by the violence and hardship that surrounded him. Instead, he made a conscious decision to share his story, hoping it would resonate with others facing similar struggles. He knew that if he could rise from these circumstances, others could too.

By the age of twenty-seven, Corey had become a father to three beautiful daughters, a role that he embraced with pride and love. Around the same time, he took on the full-time responsibility of caring for his father, who was suffering from dementia and Alzheimer's disease. This marked the beginning of a thirteen-year journey as a caregiver, up until the death of his father, a role Corey describes as both an honor and a privilege. Throughout these years, Corey balanced his duties as a father and caregiver, all while continuing his personal and professional growth.

In 2017, Corey self-published his first book, The Walk to the Light, a deeply personal narrative that shares his experiences and lessons learned from growing up in one of the most dangerous communities in America. His book is more than just a memoir—it is a guide for those seeking to break free from the cycle of hardship and adversity. Corey hopes to inspire readers by showing them that no matter how challenging their circumstances, it is possible to overcome and create a life of purpose and fulfillment.

Corey's philosophy centers on the importance of building strength in mind, body, and spirit. As a personal trainer for over fourteen years, he has helped countless individuals transform their lives through physical fitness, while also teaching them the power of mental and spiritual resilience. Corey encourages his clients to reflect on their past and present, using their experiences as fuel for personal growth and change. His holistic approach to training focuses not just on physical health, but on the mental and emotional well-being needed to overcome life's toughest challenges.

Outside of his professional work, Corey is deeply committed to giving back to his community. He serves as the Chairman of the longest-running Martin Luther King Jr. Multicultural Rally in the Bay Area, a role that allows him to promote unity and celebrate diversity in the community he loves. Corey is also passionate about organizing free meal programs for East Oakland residents, ensuring that those in need are cared for and supported.

At the core of everything Corey does is his love for his family, especially his three daughters, for whom he hopes to create a lasting legacy. In his free time, Corey enjoys spending time with his family, writing, and developing workshops that promote positivity and personal empowerment. He remains dedicated to his mission of uplifting others and using his story to create a ripple effect of change in his community and beyond.

NOTES

NOTES

Notes

Notes

NOTES

NOTES

NOTES

NOTES

Notes

NOTES

Made in the USA
Columbia, SC
16 November 2024